ISLAMIC LAWS OF
Food and Drink

ISLAMIC LAWS OF
Food and Drink

According to the rulings of Grand Ayatullah
al-Sayyid Ali al-Husseini al-Sistani

IMAM MAHDI ASSOCIATION OF MARJAEYA

Imam Mahdi Association of Marjaeya, Dearborn,
MI 48124, www.imam-us.org
© 2019 by Imam Mahdi Association of Marjaeya
All rights reserved. Published 2019.
Printed in the United States of America

ISBN-13: 978-0-9997877-1-7

Contents

I.M.A.M.'s Foreword

In the Name of Almighty Allah

May Allah shower His blessings upon
Prophet Muhammad (peace be upon him and his
progeny) and his family (peace be upon them)

Praise is for Allah, and prayers and peace be upon His prophets and messengers, especially Muhammad, who is their seal and foremost among them, and his progeny, the pure and infallible successors.

It is an innate part of human nature to adapt and become desensitized to aspects of life that are mundane, repetitive, and somewhat habitual (not requiring much conscious thought). As such, we often forget how important some of these seemingly inconsequential actions may be and ignore the role and impact they have in our daily lives. There are many instances of this for every human being, ranging from very simple acts that have minimal consequences to actions that have the potential to drastically change the direction of a person's life. An example of the former could be something as trivial as applying a fragrance that we enjoy only for a few moments because our sense of smell adapts and becomes desensitized to it. In fact, we often forget about the fragrance until someone makes a remark about it, reigniting our awareness and calling our attention to it. We realize in that moment that the scent was always there, and although our awareness of it was heightened when it was first applied, we became oblivious to it because smelling a fragrance on our own body is fairly inconsequential. Now imagine an act that we repeat daily and that has a far more profound effect on our bodies and souls.

> *We had not made them such bodies that would not eat any food nor were they immortal.*

(Quran 21:8)

The impact of food and drink upon us is very much the same. However, its significance is far greater than a fragrance, because it is essential for life. Yet, we are often negligent about the role and impact of what we consume, because it is a fixed and routine necessity of life, just as a person does not [and could not possibly] routinely think about breathing. The Holy Quran has mentioned this reality, "We had not made them such bodies that would not eat any food nor were they immortal" (21:8). Perhaps, from this perspective, Allah urges humans to observe and think about their food and drink, as He says in the Holy Quran, "[*Let the human being*] think about (how We produce) his food. We send down abundant water, and allow the earth to break open to yield therein corn, grapes, vegetables, olives, dates, thickly-planted gardens, fruits, and grass, to be the means of enjoyment for you and your cattle" (80:24–32).

If we observe and become conscious of how Allah created food and water to keep us alive and well, we would be certain that this is one of Allah's miracles that we should forever be thankful for. Allah uses the future tense of "observe" to remind us of this continuous blessing that engenders within us the inclination to perpetually remember and thank Him. Furthermore, the gracious bestowal of these resources obliges us to perform our duties as His stewards on this Earth, because we were created for a much greater reason than mere consumption and enjoyment of food and drink.

To that end, humans must cultivate two different aspects of their being to be successful in this life and the hereafter, the physical or outer dimension, and the spiritual or inner dimension.

Most people today eat without realizing what they are putting into their bodies. Fast food restaurants and processed food are everywhere. Even though this kind of food is typically less nutritious and high in saturated fat, sugar, salt, and [empty] calories, people tend to consume it without realizing its impact on them.

Nevertheless, we see that the divine calls us to observe, contemplate, and choose natural and clean food and drink.

The fact that we are multidimensional underscores the importance of this directive, and the obvious bodily aspects only partially reflect the vast and significant [spiritual] components that lie within us. Allah reminds us, "In the earth there is evidence (of the Truth) within your own selves. Will you then not see?" (51:21). Hence, from the Quranic perspective, and moreover, by looking beyond the literal language of the holy text, we realize that in the verse "observe" your "food" is directing us to examine our spiritual nourishment. As such, the inner dimension requires greater attention and scrutiny because, unlike the physical body, deficits within it may potentially impact our sensibilities, emotions, and morality.

Furthermore, it becomes clear, when looking at this issue from another angle, that the significance of "food" goes beyond what we ingest. Narrations of the Ahl al-Bayt (pbut) report that Zayd al-Shahham asked Imam al-Baqir (p), the fifth infallible Imam of the Ahl al-Bayt, about the meaning of the word "food" in the verse "So let man observe his food." The Imam (p) said, "Food is knowledge; you should carefully consider from whom you acquire your knowledge."[1]

---

1. Sayyid Ali Khan al-Madani, Riyad al-salikin fi sharh sahifat Sayyid al-Sajidin, v. 1, p. 280.

Therefore, Islam's legislation on pure food and drink forms the foundational basis for all other types of consumption (such as knowledge or information). A person should acquire knowledge from reliable and truthful sources, such that it ensures peace of mind and confidence in the legitimacy of what they learn. So, just like the long-term benefits of healthy eating on the physical body, the knowledge and skills acquired by a person through sound education and experience promote advancement and refinement of character. The Commander of the Faithful, Imam Ali ibn Abi Talib (p), said, "I am amazed at the people who turn on the light to see what they eat when they want to dine in the dark but do not care about food for their mind. They do not care to illuminate their intellect with the light of knowledge to be safe from making mistakes out of ignorance and wrong beliefs."[2]

Along with a healthy body, a healthy intellect that has integrity of mind and spirit is fundamental for success in this life and the hereafter. Moreover, one of the simplest ways by which we can begin to foster this well-being is by regulating what we eat and drink according to the laws that Allah has established. Thus, this booklet contains an Islamic educational compendium of rules, guidelines, and recommendations for food, drink, and general table manners. It contains two sections.

In the first section we discuss the five Islamic laws concerning food: (1) permissible (*halal*), (2) forbidden

---

2. *Nahj al-balagha*, ch. 3, wisdom 53.

(*haram*), (3) recommended (*mustahabb*), (4) reprehensible (*makruh*), and (5) neutral (*mubah*), which is anything that is neither commanded nor prohibited by the *shariah*.

> ❝ It is Allah who has created the earth as a place
> for you to live and the sky as a dome above you.
> He has shaped you in the best form and
> has provided you with pure sustenance.
> That is Allah, your Lord.
> Blessed is Allah, the Lord of ❞
> the universe.

(*Quran 40:64*)

In the second section we discuss the Islamic etiquette of eating and drinking. This includes serving, consuming, cleaning, cleansing, blessing, invoking Allah's name on the food, and knowing how, when, and what to do.

This is a complete system that we can apply to every aspect of life. The Quran has described good food as "pure and lawful" and bad food as "impure and unlawful." This description is enough to emphasize its importance and impact on the spirit and body. Allah says, "Those who follow the Messenger, the illiterate Prophet, (not conventionally educated), whose description they find written in the Torah and the Gospel. He (the Messenger) enjoins them to do good and forbids them to do all that is unlawful, makes lawful for them all that is pure and unlawful all that is filthy, and removes their burdens and the entanglements in which they are involved. Those who believe in him, honor and help him and follow the light which is sent down to him will have everlasting happiness" (Quran 7:157). In addition to mentioning "pure and lawful" and "impure and unlawful" (permissible and forbidden) foods and drinks, Allah emphasizes the significant positive and negative impacts of both. Allah says, "It is Allah who has created the earth as a place for you to live and the sky as a dome above you. He has shaped you in the best form and has provided you with pure sustenance. This is Allah, your Lord. Blessed is Allah, the Lord of the universe" (Quran 40:64). Thus, by virtue of the fact that He created us in the best form, Allah also required the availability of pure sustenance so that we can stay morally, materially, spiritually, and physically healthy.

We ask Allah to let this work be a useful tool for Muslims, especially the younger generation, to learn the permissible (*halal*) and forbidden (*haram*) foods and drinks, because today's markets have many forbidden items, as well as permissible items that contain forbidden ingredients. In addition, we hope that the reader simultaneously develops healthy and clean eating habits given that it is the way of Islam. We ask Allah, the Almighty to accept this work as purely to Him for the benefit of Islam and Muslims living in the West, and that it becomes a source of positive reformation in terms of our spiritual and physical food. "Believers, eat from the good things that We have given

you and give thanks to Allah, if you worship only Him"
(Quran 2:172).

Sayyid M. B. Kashmiri
Jurist Representative
I.M.A.M.

Acknowledgments

D ear reader, before you is a precise, practical jurisprudential rules booklet that seeks to provide guidance to Muslims living in the West. We would like to extend our sincere appreciation to all those who have contributed to the preparation and processing of the materials needed to bring this booklet to light. This booklet was written in accordance with the edicts (*fatwas*) of the top religious authority of the Shia sect, His Eminence Grand Ayatullah al-Sayyid Ali al-Husseini al-Sistani (may Allah prolong his life). It derives from his books *Minhaj al-salihin* and what has been published on the official website of the office of His Eminence in the Holy City of Najaf, Iraq. We specifically would like to thank Shaykh Rizwan Arastu who has written the main part of this booklet, as well as everyone who has reviewed the contents, especially His Eminence Shaykh Muhammad Taqi Shaheedy, Sayyid Abbas Razavian, Sayyid M. B. Kashmiri, and revised and rewritten by Shaykh Dr. Mehdi Hazari. May Allah reward them for their great efforts.

I.M.A.M.

Permissibility of
Food and Drink

Chapter 1

Meat

ALL ANIMALS ARE CLASSIFIED INTO ONE OF THREE groups: sea, land, or air. The following four matters must be addressed with respect to each group:

- Which meats are permissible (halal)?
- Under what circumstances is it permissible to eat the meat of an animal? In other words, how can a *muhallal*[3] animal become *mudhakkah* (slaughtered, killed, or captured in a way that makes it halal to eat)?
- Are any parts of a mudhakkah animal haram?
- How can a Muslim be certain that the meat they are eating is mudhakkah and [therefore] halal?

---

3. A muhallal animal (such as cow) is one that is permissible (halal) to eat but only after *tadhkiyah*. Thus, the term "halal" refers to the meat of an animal that is both muhallal and mudhakkah.

SEAFOOD

Which seafood is permissible (halal)?

Among fish, only those with scales are permissible (halal). Sharks, catfish, eels, and stingrays are examples of haram fish, because they do not have scales. One should assume a fish does not have scales until they know it does.

Amphibians, reptiles, sea mammals (e.g., whales), and invertebrates (such as crustaceans [like lobster and crab], shellfish and other mollusks) are prohibited (haram), because they are not fish. Among the sea animals that are not fish, only shrimp and prawns are an exception and are permissible (halal).

How can a person make a muhallal fish mudhakkah?

A muhallal fish becomes mudhakkah if any of the following is true:

- It is caught alive and taken out of the water.
- It comes out of the water by some means and is caught alive.
- It is caught in a net while alive, even if it is dead by the time it is retrieved.

It does not matter how a person catches the live fish—by fishing rod, net, trap, or hand, nor if they catch the live fish on land (e.g., if it jumps out or is left by the tide).

The person who catches the fish does not need to be Muslim nor do they need to say *bismillah* while catching it.

Some fishermen string their fish and leave them in the water after they catch them. If the fish is strung in the same water (e.g., in the lake from which it was caught) and thereafter it dies, it is mudhakkah. If the fish is caught and then placed in a bucket of water to keep it alive and then it dies, it is not mudhakkah.

There are no requirements as to how the fish should be killed once it is caught; in fact, it need not be killed (it may die on its own after being caught) for it to be mudhakkah.

Are any parts of a mudhakkah fish prohibited (haram)?

Blood and feces must be avoided as an obligatory precaution, except for what remains inside the fish's body and what is still inside the fish's gut, respectively.

Fish eggs of a haram fish are prohibited (haram). When a person is in doubt about the origin, they are not permissible to eat.

How can Muslims be certain that a fish they are eating is permissible (halal)?

A Muslim can be certain that a fish is halal if

- they catch it themselves;

- they procure it from a Muslim;
- the fish is in the possession of a Muslim who says it is halal, or even if they act in a way that implies that it is;
- they procure it from a Muslim market even if the owner or seller is not Muslim;
- they procure it from a Muslim country;
- they procure it from a non-Muslim, if they know that it is a fish with scales and has been caught in a way that makes it mudhakkah.[4]

LAND ANIMALS

Which land animals are permissible (halal)?

Among domesticated land animals, only sheep, goats, cows (including buffalo, yaks, and other bovines), and camels are muhallal (permissible after *tadhkiyah*). Horses, donkeys, mules, and hinnies are detestable (makruh). Dogs, cats, pigs, rodents, reptiles, and amphibians are prohibited (haram).

Among wild animals, only deer, antelope, buffalo, mountain sheep, mountain goats, wild asses, and zebras are muhallal. All predators, rodents (including rabbits), reptiles, amphibians, boars, bears, apes and monkeys,

---

4. It is generally (commonly) accepted that scaled fish procured from non-Muslims or from non-Muslim markets are caught using the permissible practices/techniques explained above which makes them mudhakkah.

pachyderms (including elephants), and burrowing animals (including rodents, worms, and insects) are prohibited (haram). The only exception is locusts, which are permissible (halal).

How can a Muslim make a muhallal land animal mudhakkah?

Domesticated

A domesticated land animal must be slaughtered by a Muslim, male or female, in the following manner:

- The animal must be made to face the *qiblah* such that its face and chest are toward it if it is standing, and its throat and belly are toward it if it is lying on its side. It is permissible to consume the meat if it was not slaughtered facing the qiblah due to forgetfulness, ignorance, by mistake, or if the sect of the Muslim who slaughtered the animal does not religiously obligate it.
- The slaughterer must intend to slaughter the animal by slitting its throat.
- The slaughterer must recite Allah's name, by saying something like *bismillah, Allahu akbar, al-hamdu lillah*, or *la ilaha illallah* as they kill the animal. It is permissible to consume the meat if the slaughterer forgets to do this. But if they intentionally do not do it or are ignorant of the law, the meat will remain haram.
- The blade must be made of iron if available. If not,

then any sharp blade will do. Blades made from steel or stainless steel should not be used as a matter of obligatory precaution when an iron blade is available.

- For an animal other than a camel, the slaughterer must completely cut the esophagus, the trachea, and the two carotid arteries (*al-awdaj al-arbah*) from below the Adam's apple.

- For a camel, the slaughterer must insert the blade into the depression between the camel's throat and chest.

- Blood should exit the animal's slit or stabbed throat in a natural way.

- The animal should move, shudder, or blink as it is being slaughtered. This law applies only when it is doubtful whether the animal was alive at the time of being slaughtered; otherwise, it is not essential.

It is recommended (mustahabb) to give the animal a drink of water and to prevent any unnecessary pain to the animal by ensuring the blade is sharp and by cutting quickly.

It is detestable (makruh) to slaughter an animal you have bred and raised yourself, and to slaughter an animal in front of other animals of the same species.

WILD

A Muslim must hunt a wild animal in the following manner:

- The hunter must intend to target and kill that

animal. For example, if they intended to hunt a sheep but instead shot or struck another type of animal (such as a gazelle) by accident and it was killed, it does not become mudhakkah.

- The hunter must recite Allah's name, by saying something like *bismillah, Allahu akbar, al-hamdu lillah,* or *la ilaha illallah* before they discharge the weapon or at least before the ammunition hits the animal. It is not a problem if they forget to do this.
- The hunter must use
  - ○ a hunting dog;[5]
  - ○ something sharp (it must either have a cutting edge like a machete or a point for stabbing like a spear or arrow); or
  - ○ something blunt like a bullet, but it must at least tear the skin and penetrate the flesh (killing with blunt force is not allowed).
- The animal must be dead from the wound inflicted by the hunter by the time the hunter reaches it. If it is still alive, the hunter must slaughter it with a blade (see above). If the hunter reaches the animal while it is still alive with enough time to slaughter it, and they do not do so and it dies, then the animal is not permissible to eat.

Are any parts of a mudhakkah land animal prohibited (haram)?

The blood that exits the body when the animal is killed

---

5. There are detailed laws for hunting with a dog. Please refer to a law manual or qualified scholar for details.

is haram. Any excess blood that remains in the meat after slaughtering, beyond the normal amount, is haram.

Feces, urine, genitals, placentas, glands (including pituitary, pancreas, adrenal, thyroid, and lymph nodes), spinal cords, chains of sympathetic ganglia (nerves on either side of the spinal column), gall bladders, spleens, urinary bladders, and lenses of the eyes are prohibited (haram).

Kidneys, auricles (attached to the two atria of the heart), and blood vessels (especially the carotids) are detestable (makruh).

As far as the halal parts are concerned, it is permissible (halal) to eat them cooked or raw.

How can a Muslim be certain that a land animal they are eating is permissible (halal)?

Assume a land animal is not permissible (halal) unless

- it is known to be muhallal and mudhakkah;
- it is procured from a Muslim;
- it is procured from a Muslim market; or
- it is procured from a Muslim land.

IT IS KNOWN TO BE MUHALLAL AND MUDHAKKAH

A Muslim knows meat is permissible (halal) because they slaughtered it themselves, witnessed its slaughter, or have complete confidence in the person who is informing them that it is muhallal and mudhakkah.

Halal labels on products purchased from non-Muslim markets or lands are not valid for the establishment of permissibility. Instead, the person must [sincerely] investigate to determine permissibility, or any other way that gives them certainty, that it is mudhakkah and [therefore] halal.

IT IS PROCURED FROM A MUSLIM

In the following scenarios, a Muslim may accept the meat as permissible (halal) unless they have knowledge to the contrary.

- The meat is in the possession of a Muslim who states that it is halal, or even acts in a way that implies that it is.
- The meat is bought from a Muslim seller (such as a butcher, farmer, or shop owner).
- The meat is ordered at a Muslim restaurant.
- The meat is served by a Muslim host.

If a Muslim butcher, restaurant owner, or host states that the meat is not halal, it is prohibited (haram) to eat it.

If a Muslim investigates and finds out that the meat provided by a Muslim butcher, Muslim restaurant owner, or Muslim host is not halal, it is prohibited (haram) to eat it.

IT IS PROCURED FROM A MUSLIM MARKET

A Muslim market is defined as a market or shopping district where the stores are predominantly owned and frequented by Muslims, and where a non-Muslim store is the exception. If meat is procured from a Muslim market, it may be accepted as permissible (halal) even if the religion of the seller is not known, unless there is knowledge to the contrary (in which case it is impermissible). However, if the seller is known to be a non-Muslim, a Muslim may not automatically accept the meat as halal.

IT IS PROCURED FROM A MUSLIM LAND

A Muslim land is defined as a place where most people are Muslims. The rule of thumb for identifying such a place is that people call it a Muslim country or a Muslim region.

It does not matter if you know that the Muslim seller, the Muslim market, or the seller in the Muslim land procured the meat from a non-Muslim, a non-Muslim market, or a non-Muslim country as long as it is possible that the Muslim seller or the seller in the Muslim market or Muslim land ascertained that the meat is permissible (halal).

In all these cases, any Muslim fulfills this requirement, whether they are a Twelver Shia or from another sect.

If meat is procured from a non-Muslim, the Muslim must ascertain that it is in fact permissible (halal), and they may not take their (the non-Muslim's) word for it. For example, if a non-Muslim airline offers a "Muslim" meal, a Muslim may not take their word for it, but instead they must investigate to determine its permissibility such that they are certain it is actually permissible (halal).

Special conditions

If a muhallal animal almost exclusively eats human feces for at least two consecutive days, it becomes haram. This condition is called *jallal*, and the animal is called jallal. An animal becomes jallal only by eating human feces, not the feces of any other animal or any other *najis* (ritually impure) substance. All animals (fish, land animals, and birds) are vulnerable to this condition. A jallal animal only remains jallal if it is considered to be almost exclusively fed human feces. Once it ceases eating human feces for the religiously specified time (e.g., three days for chickens), it becomes muhallal again.

BIRDS AND OTHER ANIMALS THAT FLY

Which birds and flying animals are permissible (halal)?

All birds are muhallal except for raptors (birds of prey) and scavengers (such as vultures, crows, and buzzards). When a bird flies, if it flaps more than it glides or soars, it is muhallal, and if it glides or soars more than it flaps, it is haram. If you cannot discern whether it flaps more or glides more, it is muhallal as long as it contains at least one of the following three body parts: (1) a crop structure in the esophagus where it stores food temporarily, (2) a gizzard structure where it stores stones to grind food, or (3) a spur-long talon on its leg (like a rooster's spur). In addition, all flying animals that lack feathers are haram (e.g., bats and insects, except locusts).

How can a Muslim make a muhallal bird mudhakkah?

To make a domesticated bird mudhakkah, a person must slaughter it according to the rules for slaughtering land animals. To make a wild bird mudhakkah, hunt it according to the rules of hunting.

Are any parts of a mudhakkah bird prohibited (haram)?

The blood that exits the body when the bird is killed is prohibited (haram). The blood that remains in the meat must also be avoided as a precaution unless it is negligible. The blood found in eggs is pure (tahir) but it is prohibited to eat unless it is very minute and is absorbed in the egg. and prohibited to eat, and excrement is prohibited (haram) as well. All other parts that are prohibited (haram) in land animals must also be avoided in birds as an obligatory precaution. Eggs of haram birds are prohibited (haram).

How can a Muslim be certain that a bird they are eating is permissible (halal)?

Follow all the rules for land animals to ensure a muhallal bird is mudhakkah.

Chapter 2

Food (Non-Meat) and Drink

CLASSES OF HARAM NON-MEAT FOOD AND DRINK

THE FOLLOWING CLASSES OF NON-MEAT FOOD and drink are haram to consume, and they are explained further below:

- Anything that is impure (*najis*) or has had wet contact with an impurity (*mutanajjis*)
- Anything that is considered vile or foul
- Anything that is significantly harmful
- Clay

- Wine, beer, and any other intoxicant
- Grape juice that has bubbled, either through boiling or fermentation
- The food and drink of others without their permission

Anything that is impure (najis) or has had wet contact with an impurity (mutanajjis)

Najis substances are urine, feces, semen, corpses, meat that is not slaughtered Islamically, blood, dogs, pigs, sweat of jallal animals, wine, and beer. Only beverages such as wine and beer are najis, not other forms of alcohol that are not normally consumed orally.[6] Commonly available vanilla extract contains approximately 35 percent alcohol, thus if it is consumed as is, it would be prohibited (haram). But since a very small amount of it is used in baking, then the ratio of the alcohol will become very small (e.g., one percent) in the whole of the baked food. Since the final amount is less than three percent then there is no significant amount of it remaining (it has ceased to exist due to deterioration) and it is permissible (halal) and pure.

Non-Muslims, except People of the Book, are najis. You may eat in a restaurant owned by a non-Muslim who is not a member of the People of the Book as long as you do not know for certain that the food has come into contact with the wetness from their skin (it is touched with their wet hands).

Anything that is vile or foul

Anything that is vile or foul (such as pus and scabs) is

---

6. All alcoholic liquors and drinks that intoxicate are najis based on obligatory precaution. On the other hand, rubbing alcohol or the alcohol in perfumes or colognes is not najis. See Appendix for further details.

prohibited (haram). It is not prohibited (haram) to swallow your own mucus, phlegm, and any other secretions that enter your mouth [from the inside of the body].

Anything that is significantly harmful

Anything that is significantly harmful is haram. Examples of significantly harmful things are anything that causes death (such as poison or abortion-inducing drugs), disability (e.g., causes paralysis or blindness), addiction (if harmful), or intoxication (e.g., addictive mind-altering drugs [drugs, whether mind-altering or not, should not be used as a matter of obligatory precaution even if they do not cause significant harm]). It does not matter whether the harm is definite or potential, immediate or delayed.

It is permissible to incur a lesser harm to alleviate a greater one—for example, using medicine that has harmful side effects to cure a fatal illness. For instance, medical marijuana would only be permissible if it were the only path to treating a serious illness. (Other than medicinal usage, marijuana is not allowed as a matter of obligatory precaution.)

A harmful thing is only prohibited (haram) in terms of its potential to cause bodily harm, not in and of itself. If something is only harmful in excess but not in moderation, then it is only prohibited (haram) in excess. If something is only harmful in combination with something else but not by itself, then it is only prohibited (haram) in that combination. If something is only harmful if taken regularly but not if taken occasionally, then it is only prohibited (haram) when used regularly.

Clay

Clay is prohibited (haram) to eat, whether wet or dry. The negligible amount of dust or dirt that settles on fruits or is mixed with grains or water is allowed. It is permissible to consume a small amount (no more than the size of a chickpea) of clay from Imam Hussain's grave for its curative effects.

Sand is also prohibited (haram) based on obligatory precaution. Stone, metals, and wood are not prohibited, barring any significant harm in eating them.

Wine, beer, and any other intoxicant

Wine, beer, and any other intoxicant are haram in any amount. Vinegar is permissible (halal) even if it is made from wine, if it is understood to be the former and not the latter. It is prohibited (haram) to eat at a table or spread where wine, beer, or any other intoxicant is being consumed. Based on obligatory precaution, one must not even sit at such a table or spread.

Bubbled grape juice

Grape juice becomes haram as soon as it bubbles (whether from fermentation or from boiling). Thus, grape jam and jelly are prohibited (haram). Pasteurized grape juice is not prohibited (haram) since it is usually only heated to 145 or 163°F. Boiled grape juice becomes permissible (halal) again when two thirds of its volume evaporates or is boiled away. Cooked or boiled raisins are not prohibited (haram).

The food and drink of others without their permission

Food and drink belonging to other people may not be consumed if the owner does not allow you to eat it. You must know that the owner allows you to eat it for it to be permissible to eat. This rule applies to non-Muslim owners as well as Muslim owners.

Based on Quran 24:61, you may eat and drink what is in the houses of the following people if you do not know that they will object: your father, mother, brother, sister, paternal uncle, paternal aunt, maternal uncle, maternal aunt, friend, husband, son,[7] and anyone who has entrusted you with their keys such that you are the caretaker of their house.

﴿لَيْسَ عَلَى الْأَعْمَى حَرَجٌ وَلَا عَلَى الْأَعْرَجِ حَرَجٌ وَلَا عَلَى الْمَرِيضِ حَرَجٌ وَلَا عَلَى أَنفُسِكُمْ أَن تَأْكُلُواْ مِن بُيُوتِكُمْ أَوْ

---

7. Although this verse of the Holy Quran does not explicitly mention husband or son, there are traditions from the Ahl al-Bayt (via Zurarah [*Al-kafi*] and via Abu Hamzah al-Thumali) that indicate a wife may eat from her husband's house without permission and that a father may eat from his son's house.

بُيُوتِ ءَابَائِكُمْ أَوْ بُيُوتِ أُمَّهَاتِكُمْ أَوْ بُيُوتِ إِخْوَانِكُمْ أَوْ

بُيُوتِ أَخَوَاتِكُمْ أَوْ بُيُوتِ أَعْمَامِكُمْ أَوْ بُيُوتِ عَمَّاتِكُمْ أَوْ

بُيُوتِ أَخْوَالِكُمْ أَوْ بُيُوتِ خَالَاتِكُمْ أَوْ مَا مَلَكْتُم مَّفَاتِحَهُ أَوْ

صَدِيقِكُمْ ﴾

It is not a sin (not to segregate the table) for the blind, the lame, the sick ones, and yourselves to eat at your own homes, or the homes of your fathers, mothers, brothers, sisters, or your paternal and maternal uncles, aunts, or at the homes of your friends, and the homes with which you are entrusted.

However, if you know they dislike your consuming their food and drink, you may not do so. This rule only applies to what is in their houses and to ordinary items, not delicacies reserved for special occasions and guests.

MISCELLANEOUS ISSUES

Gelatin

Gelatin is permissible (halal) if any of the following is true:

- You do not know whether the gelatin is from a

plant [substitute] or animal source.
- You know that it is from an animal that is halal.
- You know that it is from an animal and you procure the gelatin-containing product from a Muslim, a Muslim market, or a Muslim land.[8]
- You determine that the gelatin used in food is a different substance than what is extracted from the animal (through *istihalah*, meaning that its nature is transformed).

Gelatin is prohibited (haram) if you know that it is from an animal, but you cannot verify that the animal was halal.

NOTE: Sayyid al-Sistani states generally that "It is permissible to eat gelatin if one doubts whether it has been extracted from an animal or vegetable. But if it is known that it was derived from an animal, then it is not permissible to eat without ascertaining that the animal was slaughtered according to sharia." As concerns the West specifically, given that it is commonly understood that gelatin used in foods here is almost always from an animal source then it is not permissible to consume it unless one of the four conditions (above) is verified.

---

8. If a person who is committed to following Islamic rules knows that the Muslim seller does not adhere to or care about the Islamic rules (i.e., is a *fasiq*), then they will not be able to establish contentment and certainty of the product being halal.

Cheese

Cheese is halal unless you know the enzymes used to make it are from a najis or mutanajjis substance. So, if rennet is taken from an animal that is not slaughtered in accordance with Islamic law, it is not permissible.

Chocolate liquor

Chocolate liquor is pure chocolate in its liquid form—it is *not* alcoholic at all and is halal.

Vanilla extract

Many extracts (such as vanilla and almond) contain alcohol. Commonly available vanilla extract contains approximately 35 percent alcohol; thus, it would not be permissible if it is consumed as is. But since a very small amount of it is used in baking, then the ratio of the alcohol will become very small (e.g., 1 percent) in the entire baked food. Since the final amount is less than 3 percent (approximately) then there is no significant amount of it remaining (it has ceased to exist due to deterioration or *istihlak*) and it is permissible and pure.

INFORMING OTHERS OF PROHIBITED (HARAM) FOOD AND DRINK

If a person is consuming prohibited (haram) food or drink because they are ignorant of the law (they do not know it is prohibited), they must be informed of the law. If a person is consuming prohibited (haram) food or drink, not because they are ignorant of the law, but because they do not realize that the particular food or drink they are consuming is prohibited (haram) or contains haram ingredients, they do not need to be informed.[9]

EXTENUATING CIRCUMSTANCES

It is permissible to eat or drink haram things in the following circumstances:

- Necessity dictates it—for example, if a person's life depends on it, if it is the only way to save them from a severe weakness or illness, or if a pregnant or nursing mother's child's life depends on it.
- A person is compelled by another (*ikrah*) or by fear of disclosing their faith (*taqiyyah*)—for example, someone threatens to kill or hurt them if they do not eat or drink.

Under these extenuating circumstances, a person may consume only what (the least amount) they must to relieve themselves of the circumstances.

---

9. Learning Islamic rules is an obligation on each person and not necessarily teaching; however, based on the conditions of *amr bil maruf* and *nahi a'n al-munkar* (enjoining good and forbidding evil), if there is a benefit to the unknowing person and they will accept the information then they should be told.

·············◆◆◆·············

Chapter 3

Wasting Food and Drink (*Israf*)

IT IS HARAM TO WASTE FOOD AND DRINK. Two ways of wasting are throwing away what is still useful and consuming more than you need. Verse 7:31 of the Quran reads, "Eat and drink, but do not be excessive for Allah does not love those who are excessive."

﴿وَكُلُوا وَاشْرَبُوا وَلا تُسْرِفُوا إِنَّهُ لا يُحِبُّ الْمُسْرِفِينَ﴾

SECTION
2

The Etiquette of Food and Drink

The Islamic legal code has been ordained by the Creator, who knows every detail, apparent or latent, of what is beneficial and harmful to His creation. Hence, it is a perfect system of legislation that covers every aspect of life. One of the important areas addressed within this code is the rules of eating and drinking. There have been many narrations from Prophet Muhammad and his progeny (pbut) about the ethics of eating and drinking. However, to be concise, we have only chosen certain important narrations[10] to discuss in this booklet. These include details about the various conditions of eating and drinking, the ethics related to consumption, and some specific types of food and their qualities. Lastly, we have included the social ethics of eating with family, the etiquette of hospitality, and dealing with others at the table.

---

10. All narrations (*hadith*) mentioned in the chapters of this section can be found in *Wasail al-Shia* by Shaykh al-Hurr al-Amili, vol. 16 (the volume about food and drink).

Chapter 4

Table Manners

AHL AL-BAYT (PBUT) ADVISE US TO DO THE
FOLLOWING:

- To wash both hands before eating
- To wash both hands and dry with a towel
  after eating
- For the host to be the first to begin eating
  and the last to stop
- To say *bismillah al-rahman al-rahim* before
  the meal and before every course
- To eat with the right hand
- To eat with at least three fingers,
  not just two
- To lick and suck your fingers after eating
- When eating with others, to take food
  from the side of the dish closest to you
- When eating with others, not to look at
  others' faces
- To take small morsels

- To take your time eating and sitting at the spread
- To chew your food well
- To thank Allah after eating
- To floss or pick your teeth after eating
- To pick up and eat any stray food—unless you are eating outside, for it is better to feed the stray food to the animals and birds
- To eat in the morning and evening, not in the middle of the day.
- To lie supine after eating with your right leg crossed over your left
- To begin and end the meal with salt
- To wash fruits before eating them
- Not to eat when already full
- Not to eat to your fill
- Not to eat food that is hot (in temperature)
- Not to blow on food or drink
- Once bread is placed on the spread, to begin eating and not to wait for any other food
- Not to cut bread with a knife
- Not to place bread under a dish
- Not to clean all the meat from bones
- Not to peel fruit whose peel is edible
- Not to throw away a fruit until you have completely eaten it

The impropriety of eating too much

Abu Basir reported that Imam al-Sadiq (p) said, "Eating too much is detestable."

Salih al-Naili reported that Imam al-Sadiq (p) said, "Allah hates the act of eating too much."

The impropriety of satiation and overeating

Abdullah ibn Sinan reported that Imam al-Sadiq (p) said, "Eating beyond satiation causes leprosy."

Al-Asbagh ibn Nabata reported that Imam Ali said to Imam Hasan (pbut), "Shall I teach you four qualities that will allow you to forgo medicine?" He said, "Yes." He said, "Do not eat unless you are hungry, leave the food while you still have more appetite, chew your food well, and use the restroom before you sleep. If you do these four qualities, you will forgo medicine."

The impropriety of satiation and fullness

Narrations state that Imam al-Sadiq (p) said, "Satiation is the cause of every disease except fever, which comes from [and is caused by other factors]."

Abi al-Jarud reported that Imam al-Baqir (p) said, "Nothing is more hated by Allah Almighty than a full stomach."

The impropriety of leaning on something [while reclining] when eating

Muawiyah ibn Wahhab reported that Imam al-Sadiq (p) said, "Prophet Muhammad (pbuh&hp) never leaned on his right or left side while eating [as a sign of humility toward Allah Almighty] from the day he was sent as a messenger to humanity until the day of his death."

The recommendation of picking up fallen leftovers

Al-Hasan ibn Muawiyah ibn Wahhab reported that his father said, "Once, we ate at Imam al-Sadiq's house, [after finishing the meal] and picking up the tray, he picked up what fell from it and ate it saying, 'This prevents poverty and increases offspring.'"

The impropriety of eating extremely hot food

Muhammad ibn al-Hakim reported that Imam al-Sadiq (p) said, "There is no blessing in hot food."

Al-Sukuni reported that Imam al-Sadiq (p) said that hot food was brought to Prophet Muhammad (pbuh&hp) who said, "Allah did not feed us fire, let it cool down. There will be no blessing in it and the *shaytan* will have a share [if it is hot]."

The recommendation of prolonging the duration of the meal

Kumayl ibn Ziyad reported that Imam Ali (p) told him in his will, "O Kumayl! Have great manners, help your companions live a good life, and do not be harsh to your servants. O Kumayl! Take your time when you eat so that those with whom you are eating finish their food and receive their sustenance. O Kumayl! When you are finished eating, thank Allah for the sustenance and thank Him loudly so that others hear you and thank Him too, because this will increase your reward. O Kumayl! Do not keep eating until you are full, leave some room for water and air."

The impropriety of putting one of the two legs on the other and sitting that way

Abu Basir reported that Imam al-Sadiq (p) said that Imam Ali (p) said, "If you sit down to eat, then sit with humility, and do not put one of the two legs on the other [under the body], as Allah hates this way of sitting and hates the person who does it."

The impropriety of eating, drinking, and taking anything with the left hand (without an excuse)

Jarrah al-Madaini reported that Imam al-Sadiq (p) said, "It is detestable to eat, drink, or take anything with one's left hand."

The impropriety of eating while walking (without necessity)

Abdullah ibn Sinan reported that Imam al-Sadiq (p) said, "Do not eat while walking unless it is necessary."

Chapter 5

Before and After Eating

The recommendation of invoking Allah's name and glorifying Him at the start and middle of the meal

KULAIB AL-ASADI REPORTED THAT IMAM AL-SADIQ (p) said, "If a Muslim wants to eat and he invokes Allah's name and glorifies Him, then Allah will forgive him before the first morsel reaches his mouth."

Muhammad ibn Muslim reported that Imam al-Sadiq (p) reported that Imam Ali (p) said, "Invoke Allah's name when eating, do not clamor, because food is a blessing and sustenance from Allah that we need to thank Him and glorify Him for."

Abdulrahman al-Arzami reported that Imam al-Sadiq (p) reported that Imam Ali (p) said, "Whoever invokes Allah's name at the start of eating or drinking and thanks Him at the end will not be asked about the pleasure of that food ever."

Recite the following supplication when you begin eating:

بِسمِ اللهِ والحَمدُ للهِ رَبِّ العالَمِينَ. الحَمدُ للهِ الَّذي يُطْعِمُ ولا يُطْعَمُ، ويُجِيرُ ولا يُجَارُ عليه، ويَسْتَغْنِي ويُفْتَقَرُ إليه. اللّهمّ لَكَ الحَمدُ عَلى ما رَزَقْتَنا مِن طَعَامٍ وإدامٍ، في يُسْرٍ وعَافِيَةٍ، مِن غَيْرِ كَدٍّ مِنَّا ولا مَشَقَّةٍ. بِسمِ اللهِ خَيرِ الأَسْماءِ، بسمِ اللهِ رَبِّ الأَرْضِ والسَّمَاءِ، بسمِ اللهِ الَّذي لا يَضُرُّ مَعَ اسْمِهِ شَيْءٌ فيْ الأَرْضِ ولا في السَّمَاءِ وَهُوَ السَّمِيْعُ العَلِيْمُ. اللّهمّ أَسْعِدْنا في مَطْعَمِنا هَذا بِخَيْرِهِ وأَعِذْنا مِنْ شَرِّهِ وَأَمْتِعْنا بِنَفْعِهِ وَسَلِّمْنا مِنْ ضَرِّهِ.

In the name of Allah. Praise be to Allah, Lord of all realms.

Praise be to Allah who feeds, yet is not fed; who gives sanctuary [to others], but is not given (and is not in need of) sanctuary [by others]; who is without need, but is needed by others.

O Allah, to you belongs praise for the bread and soup that you have provided for us while we have remained in ease and well-being, without having had to bear any ordeals or hardship.

In the name of Allah, the best of names. In the name of Allah, Lord of the land and sky. In the name of Allah, with whose name nothing on earth nor in the sky can cause harm. He is the All-Hearing, the All-Knowing.

O Allah! Bless us with the goodness of this food, and protect us from [any] evil [it can lead to]. Avail us of its benefit, and keep us safe from its harm.

Recite the following supplication of Imam al-Sadiq (p) when you finish eating:

الحمدُ للهِ الّذي أَطْعَمَنَا فِي جَائِعِينَ وسَقَانَا فِي ظَمْآنِينِ وَكَسَانَا فِي عَارِينَ وهَدَانَا فِي ضَالِّينَ وَحَمَلَنَا فِي رَاجِلِينَ وَآوَانَا فِي ضَاحِينَ وفَضَّلَنَا عَلَى كَثِيرٍ مِنَ العَالَمِينَ.

Praise is for Allah who has fed us from among the hungry, given us to drink from among the thirsty, clothed us from among the naked, guided us from among the lost, given us vehicles from among those who must walk, given us shelter from among those who must be in the sun, and who favored us over others in the world.

Recite the following supplication when you finish drinking:

اَلْحَمْدُ للهِ الذي سَقَانِي مَاءً عَذْباً وَلَمْ يَجْعَلْهُ مِلْحاً أُجَاجاً بِذُنُوبِي.

اَلْحَمْدُ للهِ الّذي سَقَانِي فَأَرْوَانِي وَأَعْطَانِي فَأَرْضَانِي وعَافَانِي

وَكَفَانِي. اللّهمَّ اجْعَلْنِي مِمَّنْ تَسْقِيهِ فِي الْمَعَادِ مِنْ حَوْضٍ مُحَمَّدٍ

(صَلَّى اللهُ عَلَيْهِ وَآلِهِ) وَتُسْعِدُهُ بِمُرَافَقَتِهِ، بِرَحْمَتِكَ يَا أَرْحَمَ

الرَّاحِمِيْنَ.

Praise is for Allah who gave me fresh water to drink and did not make it salty and acrid because of my sins.

Praise is for Allah who gave me water to drink and thereby quenched my thirst, who gave to me and thereby satisfied me, who gave me health and sufficed me.

O Allah! Make me among those to whom you give drink on resurrection from the pool of Muhammad—blessings be upon him and his family; and [among those whom] you bless with his company. [I ask all this] by your mercy, O Most Merciful.

Imam al-Baqir (p) reported that whenever the tray of food was picked up, Prophet Muhammad (pbuh&hp) would say, "O Allah you have multiplied, pleased, blessed, fed [us], and quenched [our thirst]. All praise belongs to Allah, He who feeds but is not fed."

Abu Hamza reported that Imam al-Sajjad (p) used to say after he ate, "All praise belongs to Allah, He who feeds us, quenches our thirst, gives us abundant sustenance, supports us, gives us shelter, and showers us with his blessings. All praise belongs to Allah, He who feeds but is not fed."

The recommendation of washing one's hands before and after eating

Abu al-Awaf al-Bajali said, "I have heard Imam al-Sadiq (p) once saying, 'Washing one's hands before and after eating increases sustenance.'"

Abu Basir reported that Imam al-Sadiq (p) said, "Washing one's hands before and after eating increases [*lifespan*], cleans clothes [by removing the leftovers], and strengthens the eyesight."

.

Chapter 6

Characteristics and Importance of Certain Food and Drinks

The recommendation of eating twenty-one red raisins every day on a clean, empty stomach

AL-SUKUNI REPORTED THAT IMAM AL-SADIQ (p) reported that Imam Ali (p) said, "Whoever starts his day by eating twenty-one red raisins will not feel ill, except the illness of death, Allah willing."

The recommendation of starting and ending the food with salt

Zurara reported that Imam al-Sadiq (p) reported that Prophet Muhammad (pbuh&hp) told Imam Ali (p), "O Ali, start your meal and end it by taking some salt, for a man who takes salt before and after his meals is saved from seventy types of diseases, a minor one being leprosy."

Chapter 7

The Importance and Ethics of Hospitality and Serving Food to Others

The recommendation of having food with one's family

MASMA REPORTED THAT IMAM AL-SADIQ (P) REPORTED THAT Prophet Muhammad (pbuh&hp) said, "A man who gathers his family, eats with them, [all] invoke the name of Allah at the start of the meal, and [all] glorify Him at the end, he and his family will be forgiven."

The recommendation of honoring guests

A man came to Prophet Muhammed (pbuh&hp) and said, "I perform ablution, pray (*salah*), give charity (*zakah*), and honor my guests from the bottom of my heart. Prophet Muhammed (pbuh&hp) replied, "You will never be in hellfire, and Allah has freed you from stinginess, if you were so." And then he forbade people from going beyond their means [financially and practically] for their guests such that it becomes a hardship.

The recommendation of serving food to others

Abdullah ibn Qasim al-Jafari reported that Imam al-Sadiq (p) reported that Prophet Muhammad (pbuh&hp) said, "The best of you is the one who serves food to others, greets them, and prays while people are sleeping."

Abu al-Jarud reported that Imam al-Baqir (p) said, "The best deed toward Allah is making others happy, serving them food [*until they are satisfied*], and helping them pay their debts."

The recommendation of gathering and eating food with believers

Imam al-Sadiq (p) reported that Prophet Muhammad (pbuh&hp) said, "A complete and perfect food is the one that has these three qualities: permissibility (halal), multiple people are eating from it, and Allah's name was invoked on it at the start of the meal, and His name was glorified at the end."

Ghiath ibn Ibrahim reported that Imam al-Sadiq (p) reported that Prophet Muhammad (pbuh&hp) said, "A person's meal is enough for two, two people's meal is enough for three, and three people's meal is enough for four."[11]

---

11. The meaning of this tradition is that one should not be stingy counting people's morsels, because Allah is the one who blesses the food.

Dawud ibn al-Numan reported that Hussain ibn Ali reported that Imam al-Sadiq (p) said, "Allah has granted heaven for a man who feeds ten Muslims."

The recommendation of accepting believers' invitations

Ishaq ibn Zayd reported that Imam al-Sadiq (p) said, "The right of your Muslim [brother] is that you accept his invitation."

Mualla ibn Khunis reported that Imam al-Sadiq (p) said, "It is required to accept your Muslim brother's invitation."

It was narrated that Prophet Muhammad (pbuh&hp) said, "A poor and weak man is the one whom his brother invites and he refuses for no reason."

The recommendation of accepting a believer's invitation and eating with them even if one is fasting (mustahabb fast)

Hussain ibn Hammad reported that Imam al-Sadiq (p) said, "If your brother asked you to eat and you were fasting [a recommended fast], then eat and never let him insist and swear by the name of Allah."

The recommendation of eating from the food before you

Abu Khadija reported that Imam al-Sadiq (p) said,

"Every man should eat from the food before him and not take anything from others."

The recommendation of exchanging gifts among each other

Al-Sukuni reported that Imam al-Sadiq (p) reported that Prophet Muhammad (pbuh&hp) said, "One should accept his brother's gift [of food] and offer him a gift in return."

The prohibition of serving food for status and reputation

In *Ikab al-amal*, Muhammad ibn Ali ibn al-Hussain reported that Prophet Muhammad (pbuh&hp) said, "If one serves food for his status and reputation (just to elevate it), Allah will feed him from hellfire, and that food will turn into fire in his stomach until he is judged among people."

The recommendation of accepting the invitation of poor people and inviting them with hospitality

Al-Ayyashi mentioned in his exegesis that Masada reported that Imam al-Sajjad (p) passed by some poor people while they were eating some pieces of bread. They said to him, "Please join us O grandson of Prophet Muhammad." He folded his leg and joined them reciting the following verse of the Holy Quran: "He does not like the proud ones" (16:23). Then he said,

"I accepted your invitation, now you must accept mine, so please come and eat with me." They agreed and said, "Yes, O grandson of Prophet Muhammad," and they walked with him to his house. Then he ordered his wife al-Rabab to bring the food that they had saved.

The recommendation of serving food for the poor and non-poor

Abu Hamza reported that Imam al-Sajjad (p) said, "If a believer feeds another believer who is hungry, Allah will feed him fruits from heaven. If someone gives water to another thirsty believer, Allah will quench his thirst from the water of heaven [sealed wine]."

Abu Shibl reported that Imam al-Sadiq (p) said, "I do not see a thing more preferable to Allah after visiting a believer excepting feeding him. It is a right that Allah has granted to anyone who feeds a believer, that is to feed him from the fruits of heaven."

The disapproval of separately serving food for servants

Abdullah ibn al-Salt reported that a man from Balkh[12] said, "I was traveling with Imam al-Rida (p) to Khurasan. One day he invited everyone to have food with him including his servants, so I said, 'Why not offer them a separate table spread [with food]?' The

---

12. [Balkh was an ancient city in what is now northern Afghanistan—Trans.]

Imam replied, 'No, Allah is one, our mother is one, our father is one, and Allah rewards those who do good with the best [of rewards].'"

Ibrahim ibn al-Abbas reported that if a table spread [with food] was served to Imam al-Rida (p), then he would order his servants to sit down with him, even his guard and wrangler.

The recommendation of serving food to someone experiencing a tragic event and sending them food for three days

Hisham ibn Salim reported that Imam al-Sadiq (p) said, "When Jafar ibn Abu Talib was killed, Prophet Muhammad (pbuh&hp) ordered Fatimah to take food and give it to Asma bint Umays for three days [when her husband Jaffar at-Tayyar was martyred], and to keep her company for three days, in which it became a sunnah [prophetic tradition]."

Appendix

Additional Details on Certain Foods and Select Ingredients

Introduction

The jurists (may Allah have mercy on those passed and preserve the ones who are present) draw evidence and details from specific Quranic texts and narrations to address many rulings pertaining to food and drink. Permissible or halal foods are those that are allowed for consumption under Islamic law, whereas haram foods are those that are prohibited or forbidden.

Meats fall into the following categories:

- Meats that are essentially pure (muhallal), but permissibility to consume them requires that they are slaughtered in the religiously appropriate manner (in the name of Allah with the necessary conditions). These include many of the meats of wild terrestrial and avian animals, such as cattle, goats, sheep, chickens, pelicans, and other such animals. Dead animals (that died prior to slaughtering) are not permissible for consumption.

- Meats that are essentially impure (*najis al-ayn*);

no part of these things may be consumed at all
(e.g., pork products or derivatives).

- Meats that are essentially pure (*tahirat al-asl*) but
  prohibited to consume like predatory or
  carnivorous animals (such as lions or leopards)
  and certain animals taken from the sea (such as
  crab, lobster, eel, catfish, or sharks) except fish
  with scales and shrimp, which are considered
  permissible. As far as sushi is concerned, there is
  no problem in consuming it if the uncooked fish
  or seafood being used is religiously permissible.

Drinks fall into the following categories:

- Drinks that are permissible outright like water
  and fruit juices; all are considered pure and
  permissible to consume.

- Drinks that are permissible in their original form
  but become prohibited [due to certain changes];
  for example, grape juice, which becomes wine
  (*khamr*) upon boiling and fermentation and is thus
  prohibited to consume. This latter prohibited
  form continues to be forbidden until one-third of
  it is boiled off.

- Alcohols, like those used in certain medicines,
  condiments and sauces, and other than
  intoxicating drinks like wine and beer, are pure
  (*tahir*) but are prohibited to consume if they reach
  the religiously specified limit of intoxication (e.g.,

greater than 3 percent [approximately]).[13]
Hence, if the percentage of alcohol in a food or drink exceeds 3 percent (approximately) and the person consuming it can become intoxicated by it, then it is considered intoxicating according to Islamic law and prohibited to consume.

- Drinks that are essentially prohibited [and impure] like wine; upon contact, even a small quantity of these make any utensil, food, or drink ritually impure (najis). The alcohol content in intoxicating alcoholic beverages typically ranges from 1–20 percent.

Certain prohibited ingredients and food additives, some of which are not easily discernible, are commonly encountered and may pose a challenge to those seeking to determine permissibility or prohibition. These ingredients are added to canned foods, sweets, pastries, refreshments, medicines, and other types of food. They may be divided into six types.

---

13. The 3 percent limit of intoxication is an approximate level proposed by Grand Ayatollah Sayyid Sistani. It should not be considered a standard for every person for the very reason that some individuals might become intoxicated by alcohol concentrations less than 3 percent, for example 2 percent, in which case the latter becomes prohibited. Accordingly, a person may not become intoxicated by alcohol concentrations above 3 percent. Yet, foods and drinks containing alcohol should be avoided in general, because the alcohol concentration is usually not known, and more importantly a person does not know the concentration of alcohol at which he or she will become intoxicated.

Food preservatives

Food preservatives are substances typically derived from vegetable or non-animal chemical sources. They are used to prevent the rotting and decomposition of foods and beverages; these are permissible to consume.

Food coloring

Food coloring, or color additives, are natural (from vegetable or non-animal sources) or artificial chemical dyes or pigments that are used to preserve foods and drinks or to give them a certain color. They are permissible for consumption in most cases. However, even prior to adding it to a food or beverage, some food coloring contains very small quantities of alcohol (ethanol) that dissolves in it [such that the alcohol is diluted to a level that is so minute that it can no longer intoxicate] (istihlak). If the alcohol content in this food coloring is less than 3 percent (approximately), it dissolves, and it does not cause intoxication, there is no problem with consuming it. However, if the amount of alcohol in the final food product exceeds the previously mentioned percentage, then it is prohibited to consume it.

Shortening

Shortening is a type of fat that is solid at room temperature; it is used in many food industries.

Vegetable shortening and fats are permissible (halal) for consumption and are typically derived from olives, corn, soy, or other vegetable sources. Animal shortening like lard (pig fat), must be avoided and is prohibited (haram). Shortening or fats derived from cattle are permissible only if the animal was slaughtered according to Islamic laws. According to Grand Ayatollah Sayyid Ali Sistani, it is permissible to eat shortening or fats if one doubts whether it has been extracted from an animal or a vegetable.[14] But if it is known that it was derived from an animal, then it is not permissible to eat without ascertaining that the animal was slaughtered according to Islamic laws. Prohibited shortening or fats (those derived from a pig or an animal not slaughtered according to Islamic laws) are considered impure (najis) and will contaminate the whole food product, regardless of the quantity.

It is sometimes argued that these ingredients undergo transformation (istihalah) during the extraction process or during manufacturing. Indeed, transformation is one way an impure substance may be made pure as detailed in Islamic law. However, prevailing evidence indicates that these materials are extracted intact from the animal and still maintain their original chemical and physical makeup and properties even after being

---

14. It is commonly known to Muslims living in the West that the shortening predominantly used in certain food products (such as lard in refried beans) is from prohibited sources; therefore, these and other similar products should be avoided.

added to the food product. Therefore, it is not accurate and appropriate to describe this situation as having undergone transformation.

Finally, vegetable oils are generally used in the food industry more than animal oils because of their greater availability and cheaper price. As for shortening and grease, it must be checked and the source verified because, although plant sources are more common, animal by-products may be used at times.

Gelatin

Gelatin is a form of protein that is derived from animals. It is used in various food products and medicinal preparations because of its gel-forming properties. Generally, gelatin is derived from collagen, a protein found in animal skin and bone; it is often derived from pigs. Skin, bones, or anything derived from an animal permissible to be eaten is considered such (halal) only if it was slaughtered according to Islamic regulations. According to Grand Ayatollah Sayyid Ali Sistani, it is permissible to eat gelatin if one truly doubts whether it has been extracted from an animal or if it is a vegetarian gelatin substitute. Yet, most Muslims in the West know that certain foods (such as marshmallows, gummy bears, and a number of other gel-like confections) commonly contain gelatin from a prohibited animal source irrespective of the manufacturer. Hence, one should not automatically assume that all gelatin is permissible just because its source is not specified on the label. In any case, if it is known that it was derived from an animal, then it is not permissible to eat without ascertaining that the animal was slaughtered according to Islamic rules.

It may be believed that gelatin undergoes a chemical transformation (istihalah), but this is not necessarily the case. During istihalah a substance is transformed into something completely different such that it does not resemble its original form in any way and is understood by people to be something new. These conditions do not apply to gelatin, because the process that takes place on its source material (collagen) that is found in the bones and skin of the animal is nothing but a process of hydrogenation to increase the cohesion of the collagen molecule. Instead, this does not represent a transformation (istihalah) from one substance to a completely new one but rather a change in which the collagen still maintains its basic chemical properties. In any case, one issue persists, any part taken from an animal not slaughtered according to Islamic rules is ritually impure (najis) and it remains that way, and anything it touches (when mixed with other food) becomes impure as well. A prohibited gelatin is considered impure (najis) and will contaminate the whole food product, regardless of how much of it is in the food. This prohibition applies, as a matter of obligatory precaution, even if it was extracted from animal bones. If a chemical transformation (other than hydrogenation or physical alteration) occurs to the protein during the process of gelatin manufacturing, there is no problem in eating it.

Enzymes

Enzymes are catalysts used in food manufacturing. They may be produced from animal, vegetable, or microbial sources. The latter two types (vegetable and microbial) are permissible (halal). Enzymes derived from animal sources are numerous (see below). Enzymes derived from pigs and otherwise permissible animals (such as cows or goats) not slaughtered according to Islamic rules are completely prohibited (haram), whereas enzymes derived from cows, goats, and other religiously acceptable animals slaughtered according to Islamic requirements are permissible. Enzymes are typically included in foods at 0.01–0.5 percent of the composition, which is generally much less than the quantities of gelatin or shortening used in foods. However, a prohibited enzyme is considered impure (najis) and will contaminate the whole food product, regardless of the quantity used.

Below is a list of widely used enzymes, classified according to their animal sources:

Enzyme Name	Animal Source	Food Application
Animal rennet/ pepsin/chymosin/ lipase	Calf stomach and other live-stock	Cheese industry
Chymotrypsin/ trypsin	Cattle pancreas	Various food applications
Catalase	Cattle liver	Various food applications

Rennet is one of the enzymes that is produced from calf stomach and used in the cheese manufacturing industry. Once the calf is slaughtered, the stomach is removed, dried and ground into powder. The powder is then extracted with salt water and used in making cheese. If the calf is slaughtered according to Islamic requirements, the rennet is permissible (halal); otherwise, it is not.

Recently, cheese enzymes have been increasingly manufactured from microbial, rather than animal, sources due to the cheaper price; these are permissible to consume. However, some manufacturers choose not to label the enzyme source on their ingredient list. According to Grand Ayatollah Sayyid Ali Sistani, a person may treat these enzymes [only] as pure (tahir) if there is doubt about its source.

Other enzymes called cheese culture enzymes are also used in cheese manufacturing. They are extracted from milk, concentrated, and re-added to milk to ferment its sugars and transform milk into yogurt. These are permissible (halal).

Question: Enzymes remain dissolved in the water of cheese after processing, not in the cheese itself. Is it sufficient to wash the cheese with pure water more than one time so it becomes permissible to eat (knowing that it is difficult to get rid of the impurities within)? Answer: It is not permissible if it is known that it contains an animal enzyme [that is not permissible], even if it is small in quantity.

Aromatics/Aromas

Aromatics or aroma compounds add flavor to dishes. Typically, aroma compounds are herbs, spices, and fruit or vegetable-derived chemicals that are mixed with either oil, water, or alcohol (ethanol) as a base to enhance the flavor.

It is permissible to consume foods and beverages with aromatic compounds mixed with alcohol as long as the alcohol level is less than 3 percent (see footnote 13 above for details) and it dissolves in it [due to the mixing], and does not intoxicate.

If aromatics originate from meat products, the meat has to be religiously permissible (halal) or slaughtered according to Islamic rules, otherwise they may not be consumed, regardless of their quantity.

Glossary

hadith (pl. **ahadith**)(حديث/أحاديث). Sayings of the Prophet (pbuh&hp) and the imams (pbut).

halal (حلال). Permissible.

haram (حرام). Forbidden, prohibited, not allowed.

ikrah (إكراه). Compulsion.

israf (إسراف). Exceeding the limits, going past moderation, as determined by religious impermissibility, the judgment of the intellect, and societal norms.

istihalah (إستحالة). Chemical change. A transformation, as understood by the common person, of the essence of a substance that changes into another substance—for example, the flesh in the ground [gradually] changes to dust.

istihlak (استهلاك): When a very small amount of something (substance A) gets subsumed (dissolved and dissipated) in a large quantity of something else (substance B) such that substance A will be conventionally understood as ceasing to exist. For example, drinking alcohol is prohibited because it intoxicates, but if the percent composition of alcohol is less than 3 percent (approximately), like what might occur in some medicines for example, jurists say it is not prohibited, because it will be subsumed in 97 percent (of the medicine), and it has no capacity to intoxicate (i.e., this amount of intoxicant will not stop the brain from thinking). This is unlike mixtures that contain 10 percent or more alcohol, because that quantity can affect people and cause intoxication.

jallal (جَـلَّال). The condition of an otherwise muhallal animal that almost exclusively eats human feces for at least two consecutive days. An animal becomes jallal only by eating human feces, not the feces of any other animal or any other najis substance.

makruh (مكروه). A jurisprudential term meaning detestable or abominable. Although such acts are not forbidden or subject to punishment, a person who abstains from such acts will be rewarded.

mudhakkah (مذكَّى). An animal that has been slaughtered, killed, or captured in a way that makes it permissible (halal) to eat.

muhallal (مُحلَّل). An animal that is permissible to eat after tadhkiyah.

mustahabb (مستحب). A jurisprudential term meaning recommended under Islamic law. It is better to perform recommended actions than not to perform them, but they are not compulsory.

mutanajjis (متنجَّس). An item that is not normally najis

but has become najis by secondary causes, as
opposed to ayn najis (essentially impure)

najis (نجس). Ritually impure.

qiblah (قبلة). The direction towards the Holy Kabah in
Mecca.

tadhkiyah (تذكية). The process of performing animal
slaughter or capture so that it is permissible
(halal) to eat.

taqiyyah (تقيّة). Dissimulation. Concealing or disguising
one's beliefs at a time of eminent danger, whether
now or later in time, to save oneself from physical
or mental harm.

Other publications from I.M.A.M.

Available for purchase online

- ❖ Youth: Advice from Grand Ayatullah al-Sayyid Ali al-Sistani

- ❖ Islamic Laws of the Will
      by Grand Ayatullah al-Sayyid Ali al-Sistani

- ❖ Islamic Laws of Expiation
      by Grand Ayatullah Sayyid Ali al-Sistani

- ❖ Fasting: A Haven from Hellfire
      by Grand Ayatullah Sayyid Ali al-Sistani

- ❖ Shia Muslims: Our Identity, Our Vision, and the Way Forward
      by Sayyid M. B. Kashmiri

- ❖ Who Is Hussain?
      by Dr. Mehdi Saeed Hazari

Glossary

- ❖ The Illuminating Lantern:
  An Exposition of Subtleties from the Quran
      by Shaykh Habib al-Kadhimi

- ❖ Tajwid: A Guide to Qur'anic Recitation
      by Shaykh Rizwan Arastu

- ❖ God's Emissaries: Adam to Jesus
      by Shaykh Rizwan Arastu

Made in the USA
Columbia, SC
10 November 2024

45830811R00046